V is for Vanessa

Brooke Tara Webb

BookLeaf Publishing

Presentation by *BookLeaf Publishing*

Web: www.bookleafpub.com

E-mail: info@bookleafpub.com

ISBN: 9789357445276

First edition 2022

Cover Art: Brooke Webb

Illustrations: BookLeaf Publishing Illustrator

To the Dreamers, the Doers

and all of us somewhere in

between.

PREFACE

Dear Reader,

Over 21 days of poetry in September 2021, I found the more I wrote poetry daily, the more poetry I wrote in my poems, sometimes poems became pages long. Eventually, I remembered the haiku and the sonnet - and I appreciated their parameters. So despite being somewhat intimidated I had a go. In lockdown I think I learnt how to be a little more ambitious and a little bit more myself.

Thank you for thoughtfully starting to read my first collection of poems:

> I hope most encourage you,
> some challenge you,
> and at least one inspires you
> to write, dance or paint
> a little something too.

Yours truly,
Brooke Tara Webb

Instagram: @brooketwebb

Poem 1

Poetry
Poet - tree
Poet - sea
Poet - see
Poet - hear
Poet - here
We see the sea, we hear what's here, and we soar
into the poet-tree.
For Spring has begun.
So even in lockdown
let's make it
fun!

Day 2 - The River

The river runs along
an empty theatre,
empty school,
empty stadium,
yet it still runs.

With runners, wanderers,
cyclists and prams,
daily exercise calls us and
we refrain from shaking hands.

The ducks, the ibis,
pigeon, parrot,
the occasional seagull and
an evening sky full of bats,
meet us on our way,
as do the neighborhood dogs
and cats.

I wander past the playground,
under the bridge many
pigeons call home and
I ponder the beginnings of
the Powerhouse Museum and
some day its corridors full of
Treasure troves unknown.

There's a strange serenity,
even though the river's silent and
the white noise of construction
surrounds, for the river swallowed
the sky today, reflecting the sunset's
small, pink collection of
clouds.

Also, what are your thoughts of Pemulwuy
underfoot? I'm undecided. Is it
poignant street art?
or is it something
we pass by too easily?
And that speaker teacher,
by the Church Street stairs,
does it also freak you out
almost always catching you unawares?

p.s. I have a mural idea for underneath the Barry Wilde Bridge. Maybe one day I will investigate how to transform the idea into something more tangible, visible even. Mariah Calman, Charlotte Allingham, Ellen Porteus, would you consider it? Though we will need to bear in mind that it floods.

Day 3

Songs of Innocence and *Songs of Experience*
Blake, did you know which is which and why?
I see inexperience of
pain as innocence. A false security.

No rejection, no razored
words or sharp slaps
of other people's realities
across your face.

Heartache that isn't self
inflicted, or the fight or flight (or freeze)
you didn't realise kept
you always on….

Who invented the light bulb?
Graham Bell? No

He invented our chance to call
for help.
If only hotlines
didn't sometimes
make you wait so
long.

Too harsh?

Maybe you should read this one last?
Or fast?

Casting off cares,
I hope to comfort the disturbed
And disturb the comfortable.

Uncomfortable if I even use this
poem for I don't want to
trouble
the young
or the innocent
ones.

Day 3, what have you become?

Alternative Day 3 Poem

Do you know the difference
between arriving at
Sydney airport and at any
other airport in the world?
I recognise things.

If I have a window seat on
the right side of the aircraft and
it's the right time of day, the
harbour comforts me. The sunlight
glistens off the Tasman Sea and the
Harbour Bridge and Opera House are
in all their glory from above.

One day we will return to those
white oversized doves.
Be patient while we must keep
looking from the ground:
Up.

Poem 4

words words words words words words
heard heard heard heard heard
danced danced danced danced danced
moved moved moved moved moved
soothed soothed soothed soothed soothed
me you me you me you me you me

Poem 4 found at the door to:
*DIARY OF A FREELANCER**

you me you me you me you me you
soothed soothed soothed soothed soothed
moved moved moved moved moved
danced danced danced danced danced
heard heard heard heard heard
words words words words words words

* Amanda Jones (2021).

5. Father's Day 2021

Do you remember
changing the steps
out the back?
Or adding the
steps out the front?

Methodical and thoughtful,
doll houses and pirate ships.
Always remember
nothing is impossible
and practice can
help make things
perfect…

The netball hoop and
trampoline I used to
pitch to might be gone
and us kids have moved out too.
Know that we
love you
and pieces,
peaces, of you
are always with us.
Music, movies,
footy and meat pies,
a quiet calm,

a gentle presence
and there to help
us at the drop of
a sentence.

Thanks for always keeping on -
we see you,
we're here for
you, forever and
beyond.

Having steps at home might suck now
but know that we'll
never let you step
down. Step over or
around maybe… sure,
but be sure to know
that to us you have always been,
will always be,
a step above the
rest.

Rest in lockdown and
we will celebrate soon.

Thanks for everything,
thank you for all you do.

Monday 6.9.21: The Day After

Mum, I remember your pink little
TV and how even when I had my own
bed I still crept into yours. I'd
watch Agro while you sometimes
slept in and you had Bon Jovi
on the back of your door.

Do you remember eating that
melted layer of ice-cream
after we walked home with our
grocery shopping?
Or our thick, hot, vanilla custard with
Milo or cinnamon?

What about apple turnovers?
From near the station and the
chemist where we always developed
two or three rolls of film?

Back when developing film
was like sending pottery -
your clay, your creativity - to the
kiln. From your precision and your noticing
eye, your photographs are full of memories,
moments you didn't let pass us by.

Physie, Girls Brigade, Little Athletics,
Gumnut Guides, netball, dancing, dancing and
dancing some more, singing, softball, and acting
too.

City to Surf, Carols in the Domain
and the Sydney Royal Easter Show;
Tina Arena and Kylie Minogue,
always, always remind me of you.

Around the world twice
and through many ups and
downs.
I love you to the moon and stars
and back again,
I love you all year round.

The weight of glory waits for you,
as I do too,
you will always be my mum, mum,
please know this to be
true.

Thank you, too.
Thank you for being
you.

xo xo

Poem 7: Did you hear?

~~Courage~~ calls,
~~courage~~ whispers,
~~courage~~ shouts.

Weary
our rage calls,
whispers,
our rage SHOUTS!
Tears tear through
not sure what to do.

Courage calls: "Did you hear?"
Whispers: "Here"
Shouts: "LET'S GO TO...!"

While the world keeps turning,
"Courage calls to courage
everywhere"
To me,
to you.

Millicent Fawcett - Caroline Criado Perez
- Gillian Wearing.

What have we got to lose?

mw - I'll keep calling,
whispering, shouting.
Will you?

Poem 8: A WIP, Something TBC

THE

D R E A M   H - E - A - P*
a e v v o   E D R O
r a a a t   A U T L
e d l i i   L C S I
j u l v   T A T
u a a a   H T I
s t b t   I C
t e l e   O S
e   N

* A trademark, a platform, a production company? tbc - but may it become a place to share discoveries of problems we've noticed and solutions we dare to dream about.

How do we dismantle
the stability of
wealth to reconsider
the fragility of inequity?

Socialism? Democracy?
World Peace? World Provision?
I have no idea. Honestly.

But from now on
Let's not just sit here,
let's hear.

For our stories connect us whether we
like it or not.
From the air we breathe to the
sun we see
let's start fresh - let's re-imagine society.

#tomorrow's task: define society and H.E.A.P.

9. R U Ok? Day

May we be patient with our yesterdays,
present in our todays
and diligent with our tomorrows.

V is for Vanessa

V is for Vanessa. Her collection
of elbows and knees, and her
puzzle of positive, negative space.

V is for vision...
. vulnerable
. vernacular
. violent
. vaginas too.

Violet, violin, Viola, voilà!

Vexed
Perhaps I should look at
the dictionary for more...

V for vision always sticks with
me. Though, better yet, re-vision,
for even my Vanessa sits there
peacefully pondering...

Maybe we should try
to take on that pose, that
posture.
Ponder up a vacation
for vous, or vacantly vouch for

just being invariably still.
Like a vase,
like my Vanessa.

IV is four. V, five. VI six.
V + V is ten. X.

May my Vanessa,
now also become yours.

Note: This is what happens when poetry activism interrupts my sleep - thanks to Emma Watson, Rupi Kaur, Sarah Wilson and Clementine Ford (& @CuriousReadsBookClub) for some of the themes. <3

September 11th, 2021

A fountain forever falling.
Restoring, remembering, and hoping
we can be:

♪♩Here, at the start of a moment,
on the edge of the world,
where the river meets the sea♪♩*

One world, one day.
Maybe, unity.

```
          Y

          I
          I
 _________I___________
1\                   /1
1 \                 / 1
1  \               /  1
1   \             /   1
1    \           /    1
1     \         /     1
1      \       /      1
1       \     /       1
1        \   /        1
1         \ /         1
1          I          1
1          I          1
1          I          1
1          I          1
1          I          1
1          I          1
1          I          1
1          I          1
1          I          1
1          I          1
1          I          1
```

#OWTC-2021

* lyrics from *Come From Away* a musical that is still brilliant 10 years on.

** * *
* (* * *) **
**) * * (*
*) * * (**
** * *) I (* * *
* 11 *
11
11
(------11 -----)
11
#survivor-tree

////D
//// D
\I D ///D
II DD // D
I D / D
I D
___v____
#dove-oculus

Poem 12 - What was plan A?

Authority
For what cause?
God? Race? Gender? Politics?
Home.
Anger - tension
Neglect?
Insecure, insular?
Speechless yet trying not to be
Talk - for I will listen...
Aware - but feeling out of my depth
Now? how? why? I sigh,

Overwhelmed by the distance,
the distress and the difficulties
of others.

May God be with
them: both the precious and the
powerful and may we all
question the difference.

13B

13 - can you see the B
it makes? I like that.
I think it was one of
Taylor Swift's favourites when
she used to write on
her arms on tour. I
liked that too, like test
driving tattoos with texta.
Growing up Taylor was like
a long lost sister - playing
her songs on guitar and her
cds on repeat.

Now I have long lost sisters
left at our 13 in London and
our other 13 in Berlin.
Thankful for white painted bricks
and yellow front doors, and for
staircases to living spaces
so you rarely look at walls.
Spoilt with the view - their
faces, fairy floss skies,
rooftops,
and butterflies.

I'm thankful for Bs and for

13s, for friends that are
more like long lost sisters
that I left behind for a
while with the cherry blossoms,
house plants
and cheeky squirrels.

And while I’m closer to 33
than 13 these days, I’m also
thankful that the B will always be
with me
from the start and until
the end.

13 equals B : Do you see?

I Have Almost 14 Tattoo Ideas

A snowdrop - a tiny first flower of spring
and white as snow, but does it go
above the ankle, or near the hip
but below?

A book - open, possibly falling off of the
table in a Jean Metzinger painting:
Livre et pipe rouge,
my sketch study could help with the
design. But again, if I get it on the inside
of my arm which way is right?
My way or your way?
Who will look at it more?
Who is it really for?

A cross - 2cm by 1cm.
To go on the left side, of the
inside, of my wrist, sometimes beneath
my wrist watch but always an
acknowledgement of my
faith.

A quote? But which one? In full?
Or just a phrase?
Two that have lingered are:

"I'd rather learn from one bird how not to sing
than teach ten thousand stars how not to dance" -
e. e. cummings
Or the title of Daniel Tammet's book: "Every
word is a bird we teach to sing."
Maybe for across my ribs or the inside
of my right arm.

Words. In size 10
or 12 font (exact font I am
unsure) but on the
right foot dance and
the left foot sleep,
near the toes or the ankle,
I really don't know but
I still feel keen.

My brother's ideas:
Australian Map on his calf
and a Blue-jay somewhere sweet.

Undecided, maybe this Christmas
I will commit.

Oh wait- I almost forgot - a continuous
line drawing of some kind,
a face or a flower.
To "love freely" above an elbow on my arm.

And finally, a musical note could be
an option too, on the inside of a finger
on my left hand so I can try to see it
when I play my acoustic guitar. It might
give me a reason to get better
at tablature.

And an art one:
an oval paint pallet,
with flowers, on the back
my calf.

At 15

Being halfway to 30
at 15 is a ridiculous
concept. When 18
seems like it's wrapped in
freedoms you dream of,
30 is some sort of distant
blur.

At 20, teendom is left
behind but you're still
unsure and sometimes unkind:
to yourself, your body, your mind,
your peers, your parents.
And 20 has so many
different kinds:
- university student
- full time employee
- apprentice
- uncle/aunt/parent
- sibling
- in between
- at home
- at your first home away from
home with your trinkets and coffee
machine making it feel
your own.

- you might own a car
or you still might not drive.

You survive.

Sometimes with eyes wide and
open for adventure.
Sometimes eyes closed
where everything feels very
insular, insecure and insincere.

Sometimes the uncertainties
of reality,
of relationships
hit you,
hurt you, but somehow
still help you, at least you hope
they do.

You sit and pick up sticks
wondering if fetch
will actually work.

Work. It becomes a
priority and takes up
most of your time.
Sometimes for the best,
and other times just for a dime.

Seasons chime with
marriages and babies,
funerals and birthdays.

Occasionally you know
exactly what to say.

You might begin to
feel an ease,
a sort of contentment
that comes and goes
and you expect the
unexpected, realising
that it's all part of the
show, the dance.

That romance trance that
comes your way,
by chance it lasts or
by circumstances it passes.

Seasons, reasons.

One foot after another,
one foot in front of the other,
other,
        other,
                other.

At 15, I didn’t think I’d love
painting so much or
feel peace and present
writing poetry.

At 30+, I’m pleased that
my musical impulse of
youthfulness still lingers
and I embrace never
ceasing to break out into a song
or a twirl from time to
time.

I spend time. I waste time - wisely and
unwisely…
ruly and unruly.

Perhaps I pause more
and really, I should.

For that door from 15
to 30 wasn’t a trap
more like a tornado,
kind of wonderful,
now as I look back.

I’m thankful, thoughtful and yet
honestly somewhat helpless.

But gratefully hopefulness
always leads the way.

(The Way, the Truth, the Life)

From halfway to 30, I'm now
part way to everything else.
Part way to -
myself.

My "Something I'm made of wants to tell a story" shirt arrived yesterday. It's by sisters Tess Guinery and Sharee Karlin. So I'm more determined to give it a try.

Also, thankful to my year 10 Geography Class who submitted some of their ideas of what they hope their life may be like at 35. As Mariah Calman would say: "Be who you needed when you were younger".

But SLEEP - since you're falling asleep midsenten…

This Artist's Way To Her Why

Today I start uncomfortably calling
myself an artist, a painter,
a creatr.
Over the years I have slowly,
ever so slowly, come to
call myself a dancer,
a teacher, a writer, only from time to time…
But friend, sister or daughter
normally come much easier.

But to be an artist…
and why?
I guess for years I would sing
about painting a sunset or
sunrise and then one day
I tried.

My heart explodes at colour,
albeit hesitantly.
I never knew they were warm
and cool. From 6 primary colours
and some marvelous titanium white I
explore -
acrylics mostly, watercolour occasionally
and my mind is constantly boggled by
what we can do with Procreate.

For me art is tasting
time.
I hear Holy Spirit whispers
as I create a charcoal
sketch
and through it
learn to rush to
rest.
Rest is my why. Well,
one of them, to learn is too;
to see the sea and sky in dappled
colours. To paint poetry is my
why.
I've wandered with
Wordsworth, painted
daffodils and now fresh
ones from my balcony hope
to become timeless too.

I buy perishables like
pineapples to make sure
I paint something;
and all too often I
see spaces with creative
potential to transform into an
exhibition, an exploration.
Or random walls along my commute
or walls visible from
my apartment windows, won't take too

long for me to mentally plan
a mural or two: Parramatta, I’ve got my
sights set on you. (and Fulham, I’ll come
back for you).

To paint people and petals;
circles and triangles.
To paint my dear, sweet
Vanessa, and ponder:
background colours and
clever titles.

Myself as an artist,
an artist as my self,
is in faith.
As I contemplate:
My why?
My what?
My how?
My who?
With the lovely
and wonderful
United ArtSpace's view.
5 workshops, 7 keys
and 12 weeks of
lockdown life,
maybe I’ve finally
realised I’ve
always been:

By The Way -
The Artist's Way
of life.

That [seven-story mountain] path, a spiral path, is how I think of the Artist's Way. As we pursue climbing it, we circle back on the same views, over and over, at slightly different altitudes… Growth is a spiral process, doubling back on itself, reassessing and regrouping. … [so climb] in the spirit of reparation - not to others, but to ourselves.

> - Cameron, J. (2002). *The artist's way: A spiritual path to higher creativity.* New York: J.P. Tarcher/Putnam (pp.203-204).

17 Syllables

Cherry blossoms grew
out my window, pink petals,
adored, float to floor.

Rounding Up

"When my life became unmoored by sorrow" [1]
I attempted performance art.
Augusto Boal's *Theatre of the*
Oppressed.

♪♩Say it's only a paper moon,
sailing over a cardboard sea,
but it wouldn't be make believe if
you believed in me.♪♩ [2]

Blanche sings this in *A Streetcar Named*
Desire - but I forget if
Cate Blanchet did. [3] I just remember
adoring seeing her in the
flesh - but wishing it was with

---

[1] Quote from Wild by Cheryl Strayed. I started reading it yesterday and have wanted to ever since learning it was the first book adaption Reece Witherspoon chose to produce herself.

[2] Song lyrics from It's only a paper moon I learnt at my ACTT Activate drama class in 2005 which added depth of understanding to when I studied Streetcar as a HSC drama text.

[3] Sydney Theatre Company 2009 Production of A Streetcar Named Desire directed by Liv Ullmann and starred Cate Blanchette

her Australian accent. I don't know
many Australian plays.
This song was: round 1.

Round 2: was a dance (and a song)
by night and by day. I wish I
knew where it was, why it was, what
it was, for I'd never been
there before nor have I since.
It was brilliant even if unsuccessful…
but I still remember the sunrise, like
dancers out of my wildest dreams.

Round 3: was a yelling match.
My spirit to theirs.

Round 4: I sort of surrendered early,
caught off guard and unaware
of what on earth to do.

Round 5: I'm still deciding - observing
roads not taken and possibly
pouring sand into the ones I have.
For I am spiralling up- Post Traumatic
Growth - and this trauma is not
my fault - but it is my
Responsibility [4] .

---

[4] How to Glow Up In Your Business with Dr Marion Piper (September, 2021). StartUp Creative Podcast on Dr Piper's

So until one day when I spiral up the
NYC Guggenheim again with my spin
top[5] and sketch book in hand. I'll try not
to undermine the
sorrow - unmoor it instead - and
sail off to transform
oceans of words still
left unsaid.

Watch out - I think this next
round is freeing…

---

research on creative resilience and Post Traumatic Growth - the Spiral Up. Including Beth Moore's quote: Trauma is not my fault but it is my responsibility.

[5] The best souvenir from my 2019 trip to the NYC Guggenheim is my spin top - that architecture and art travels with me as I keep rounding UP.

19 Elephants in our small apartment room

I - The Start of Lockdown

Covid 19
We thought you were
gone. Zero cases for days, and then weeks,
months even, only for a pilot driving around
town to
bring all of NSW tumbling down.

From Bondi to Fairfield,
Bunnings to KMart.
This invisible virus forces
us apart to isolate,
hibernate, remember it does
not discriminate.

It just brings out our
hate.
Hate for sickness and
losing lives.
Hate for financial pressures
and our lifestyles being minimised.

Covid 19. We're now 20 months
in, online learning again

thinking why did it have
to begin…

Dreaming of the end…
Vaccines, will they help
us win?

- 15.7.21

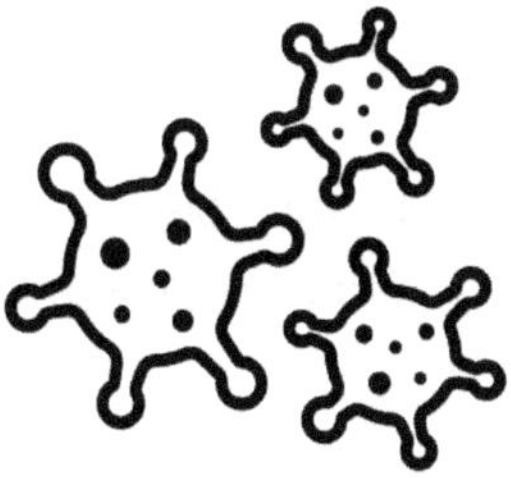

II - The Middle of Lockdown

Soonisms* from Sydney in August 2021

Soon we will get to the theatre again. "I'm willing to wait for it!" *Hamilton*!
Soon we can meet up for brunch with a reservation and no reservations about our safety or the safety of others.
Soon we can be in the classroom together again and not know how to interrupt all the chatter because somehow we've missed all the small talk and the things in between learning that makes school school.
Soon we will get to laugh with, and at, each other again.
Soon we can swim again, the repetition of each stroke calming and encouraging endorphins and improvements.
Soon we can have family bbqs.
Soon we can swap books in person and not by post.
Soon we can share a meal on birthdays rather than a zoom call.
Soon we can sneeze and not freak out too much although maybe we still will.

Soon things will change, but some things won't.
Loved ones lost, and the little ones gained but
we are yet to meet.

Soon we will hug, hug a little longer to make up
for all this time.

Soon and very soon I'll be seeing you.
So stay safe, stay sensible
and let's hold on to
our soons.

*What I thought a poem by Barton Smocks titled *Soonisms* could be about. Mine is in light of our lockdown and the delay in our redefining of normal.

III - The End of Lockdown

20. Process Poem*

I dance with words and write with moves to soothe.
I follow my heart and wander around
In and out of consciousness - how smooth?
I try to figure out, to understand sound.

Silence deafens, emotions compound - I write:
what's inside, outside, and upside down.
I dance until I feel - left right left right.
I linger, I wait, awestruck by His crown.

His Glory, mystery, numbers, surround me.
I puzzle, improvise, and surrender.
I piece together the stars, sky and sea.
I'm less a poet and more a sender.

Yet reading is breathing in, poetry out
Melodies paint movements so music shouts.

*my first attempt at a sonnet as I discussed in my preface, so your feedback is welcome. I'm always leaning in, always learning out. I hope this delights the dancers, the poets, and the painters, and may many more dare to come out and have a go too. <3

Leaves

II

Leaves leave gracefully
leaving leaves faithfully
falling freely feeling
leafy
until leaves are left
everywhere – from left to
right - Right?

27/03/2015

Thank you to BookLeaf Publishing

Thank you to *BookLeaf Publishing* and their *21 Days Writing Challenge*. It has been a comforting constant for our Sydney lockdown and thankfully it couldn't get cancelled like my *Hamilton* tickets or a creative writing workshop. Also, I wanted to note that I published this last poem on a poetry blog of mine so long ago, and I am thankful that this challenge has revived my love of poetry and the practice of writing daily. My blog with so few poems seems to reveal that perhaps print, and the prospect of tangibly sharing a compilation of my work, is more my style. So thank you again to *BookLeaf Publishing*, nature references always get me, and thanks to you, the reader, for joining me on the journey: 21 days of poetry in September 2021.

ACKNOWLEDGEMENT

Thank you to all of you that know who you are
to me
and all of you that still may not.
For inspiration, encouragement,
grit, and wisdom.

Thank you to all of you for being here
from day dot.

Also, stay in touch, especially if you might want to see Vanessa take on another life in my *Vanessa Art Series* coming Spring 2022. May pausing and pondering become a reve-lation.

My old poetry blog that I might revive:
https://brooketarawebb.blogspot.com
Instagram: @brooketwebb

www.ingramcontent.com/pod-product-compliance
Lightning Source LLC
Chambersburg PA
CBHW051738130826
49812CB00033B/911
* 9 7 8 9 3 5 7 4 4 5 2 7 6 *